I love that you're my

 **Husband**

because

I Love You Because Books
www.riverbreezepress.com

To My Husband

Love, _Wifey_

Date: _8-15-19_

I remember when we

_____

You make me feel special when

_____

You have brought more

_____

into my life

I love when you tell me about

_____

I love when we

_____

together

You taught me how to

_____

I know you love me because

_____

I love that we have
the same

_____

I am amazed at your ability to

_____

You have really sexy

_____

You make me laugh when you

_____

I wish I had more time to

_____

with you

You have
inspired me to

_____

If I could give you anything it would be

_____

I would love to go

_____

with you

You are
there for me when

_____

I love you because you are

_____

47878508R00028

Made in the USA
Lexington, KY
13 August 2019